CW00482124

PORTHMADOG
TO
BLAENAU

Vic Mitchell and Keith Smith

MP Middleton Press

First published April 1995

ISBN 1 873793 50 2

Design - Deborah Goodridge

Published by Middleton Press
          Easebourne Lane
          Midhurst
          West Sussex
          GU29 9AZ
          Tel: 01730 813169
          Fax: 01730 812601

Printed & bound by Biddles Ltd,
          Guildford and Kings Lynn

INDEX

PLACE NAMES

During the nineteenth century great efforts were made by outsiders to anglicise Wales, resulting in confusion in the spelling of place names. For historical accuracy and consistency, the form used by the railways in the period covered by this book is generally adopted.

The Festiniog Railway's Act of Parliament was passed with only one "F" and so the railway's name cannot easily be changed, although it is now marketed with two.

In giving a guide to pronunciation, it must be assumed that the reader has heard the unique Welsh sound of "ll". The places are listed in journey order.

Portmadoc was renamed Porthmadog in 1974 despite having been built and named by Mr W.A.Madocks MP. The Welsh Prince Madog has gained fame for reputedly sailing to North America from a site north of the town, long before it existed. Both spellings are used in this album, depending on the period under discussion.

Unfortunately, the three railways in Porthmadog still fail to make a distinction between their stations, as was widely practised in the nineteenth century. Porthmadog North and Porthmadog Harbour would be helpful to visitors, authors and their readers.

Minffordd	Mean-forth
Penrhyn	Pen-reen
Tan-y-bwlch	Tan-er-boolk
Dduallt	Thee-a*ll*t
Llyn Ystradau	*Ll*in erstradii
Tanygrisiau	Tan-er-grish-yah
Blaenau	Bly-nigh

ACKNOWLEDGEMENTS

To those who have provided the photographs we express our deep gratitude, particularly to so many who have given much information and additional help at the same time. We are also grateful for the assistance given by J.Hewett (and indirectly others who have helped to compile the FR Chronology), D.F.Gunning, N.Pearce, Mr D. and Dr.S.Salter, and M.Seymour (FR Company Archivist and producer of the diagrams in this album).

Our sincere thanks for checking the manuscript for historical accuracy go to A.G.W.Garraway MBE, N.F.Gurley, A.Heywood, A.Ll.Lambert, M.Seymour and D.Wilson.

GEOGRAPHICAL SETTING

Portmadoc and its harbour were established in the 1820s, as the construction of the embankment or Cob resulted in the Afon Glaslyn scouring a deep channel near the tidal sluices. The port was suitable for the ships of the period and the town expanded as a result of the increasing trade, being laid out in a grid-iron pattern, as was common in new towns of industrial Britain.

The FR terminus is at the Harbour and its first mile traverses the level Cob. Thereafter the line was on a continuous rising gradient. To Penrhyndeudraeth the route is along a tapering finger of high ground that separates the valleys of the Glaslyn and the Dwyryd, the latter river being the main feature of the Vale of Ffestiniog. By Dduallt, the line is over 500ft above the valley floor and passes through part of the Moelwyn mountain range by means of a tunnel. In this vicinity granite was of economic importance, but the predominant mineral worked from here northwards is slate of high quality.

From Tanygrisiau the route runs up the valley of the Afon Barlwyd. It is in the urban area of Blaenau Ffestiniog for its final mile, being overshadowed by mountains and slate rubbish tips. The town is one of the highest in Wales at over 700ft above sea level.

The track diagrams herein are as in 1954.

HISTORICAL BACKGROUND

An Act of Parliament was obtained in 1832 for the construction of the line, which was intended to facilitate the conveyance of slates from the quarries of the Blaenau Ffestiniog district to the shipping wharves at the then new town of Portmadoc. Gravity and horses were to be the main sources of motive power on the route, which was (six years after opening) on a continuous down gradient to the sea and nearly 14 miles in length.

Traffic commenced in 1836 and increased greatly, necessitating the replacement of the horses by steam locomotives in 1863 for hauling the empty slate wagons back to the quarries. Passenger traffic started officially in 1865.

The line prospered as a general carrier, double engines being introduced in 1869 to increase capacity. Blaenau Ffestiniog was reached by the London & North Western Railway in 1879 and by the Great Western Railway in 1882. By the end of the century, these factors combined with a decreasing demand for slate, resulted in substantially reduced revenue for the FR.

The demands of World War I reduced the maintenance of the line and its ability to meet the competition of the emerging road transport industry after 1918. Despite the development of tourism between the wars and the hopes of expanding this traffic in association with the 1923 Welsh Highland Railway, the company's fortunes continued to decline.

World War II resulted in the cessation of passenger services on 15th September 1939 but slate trains continued until 1st August 1946.

A number of people made abortive attempts to revive the decaying railway but it was the enterprise of a young man, Leonard Heath Humphrys who called a meeting in Bristol in 1951, which led to the formation of the Festiniog Railway Society. Mr Alan Pegler succeeded in gaining control of the historic company on 24th June 1954 when new directors were appointed and the controlling interest was passed to a trust. The complexity of the story of this period is illustrated by the diagram on the page after next.

Mr Allan Garraway became manager in June 1955 and general manager from 1958 to 1983. With the support of a small staff and many FRS members, passengers services were restarted from Portmadoc as follows:

To	Boston Lodge	23 July 1955
	Minffordd	19 May 1956
	Penrhyn	20 April 1957
	Tan-y-bwlch	5 April 1958
	Dduallt	6 April 1968
	Llyn Ystradau	25 June 1977
	Tanygrisiau	24 June 1978
	Blaenau Ffestiniog	25 May 1982

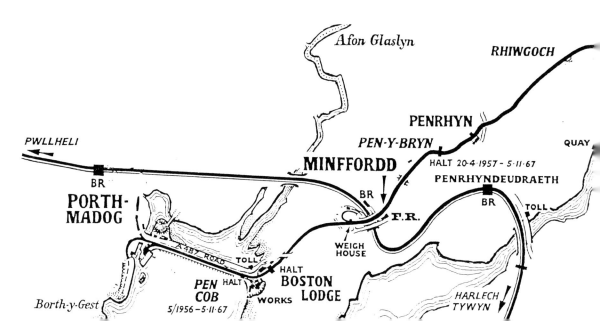

The prolonged legal battle to obtain compensation for the cost of reinstatement of the line submerged under a lake forming the lower part of a pumped storage hydro-electric system has been chronicled many times. The successful outcome of the negotiations for a deviation is illustrated herein.

The history of the rolling stock is summarised in the FR *Traveller's Guide*.

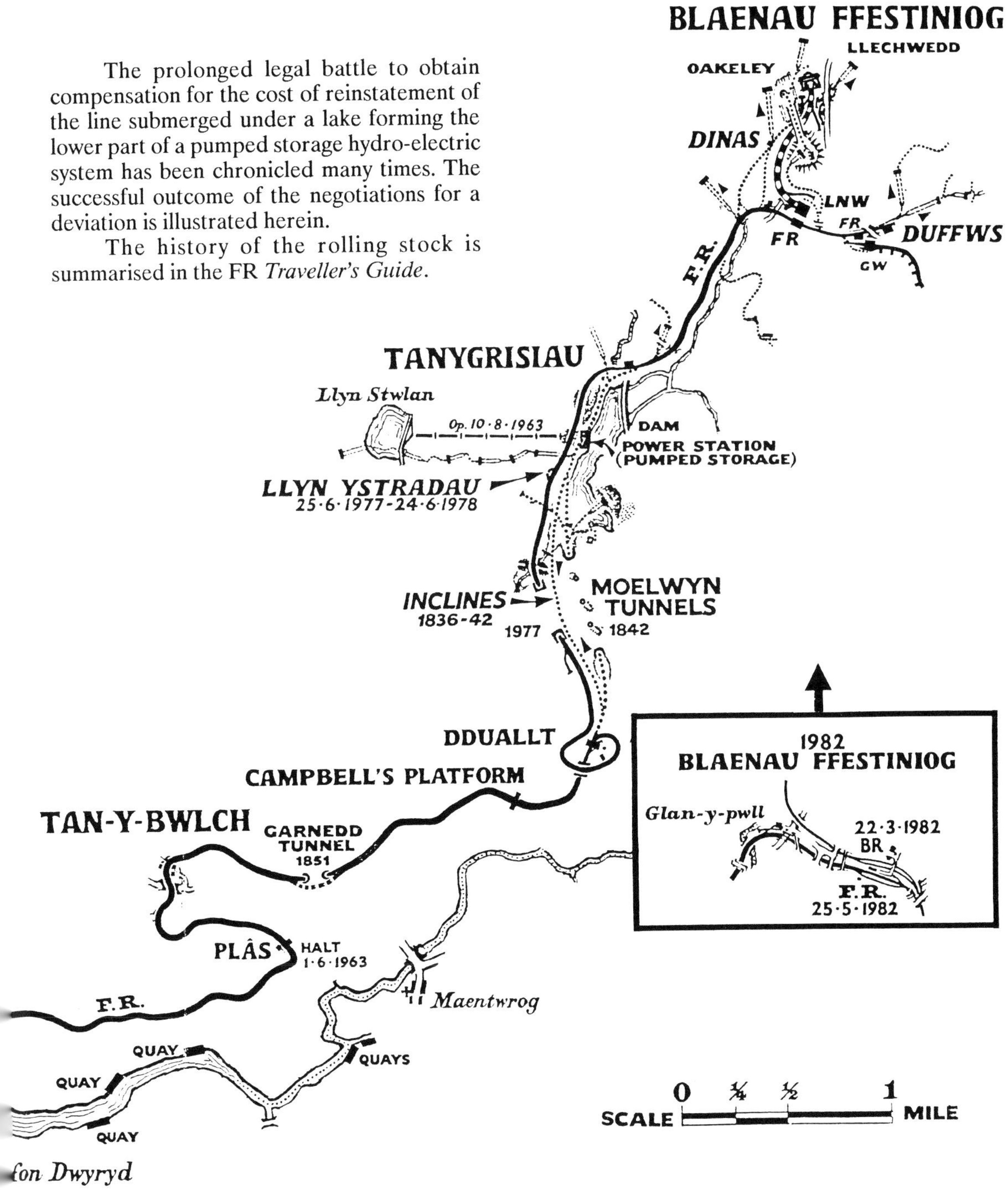

BLAENAU FFESTINIOG

LLECHWEDD

OAKELEY

DINAS

F.R.

LNW

FR

FR

DUFFWS

GW

TANYGRISIAU

Llyn Stwlan

Op. 10·8·1963

DAM
POWER STATION
(PUMPED STORAGE)

LLYN YSTRADAU
25·6·1977-24·6·1978

INCLINES
1836-42   1977

**MOELWYN
TUNNELS**
1842

DDUALLT

CAMPBELL'S PLATFORM

TAN-Y-BWLCH   GARNEDD
TUNNEL
1851

1982
BLAENAU FFESTINIOG

Glan-y-pwll
22·3·1982
BR

F.R.
25·5·1982

PLÂS   HALT
1·6·1963

F.R.   *Maentwrog*

QUAY

QUAY   QUAYS

QUAY

0   ¼   ½   1
SCALE ▭▬▭▬▭ MILE

fon Dwyryd

KEY

C	Crane	SP	Signal post
ES	Engine shed	TT	Turntable
GS	Goods shed	WB	Weigh-bridge
LC	Level crossing	WT	Water tank
SB	Signal box		

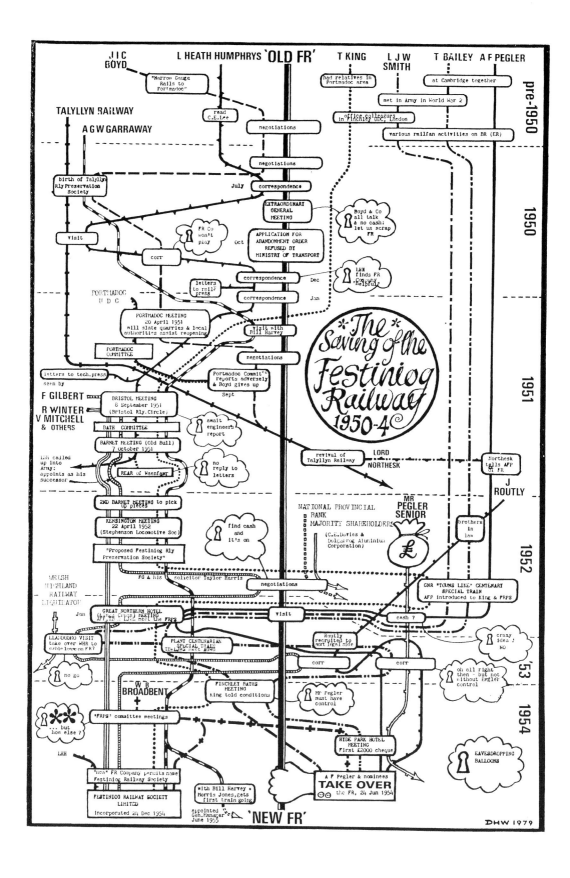

The Saving of the Festiniog Railway 1950-4

DHW 1979

PASSENGER SERVICES

The peak summer weekday timetables for the first years of FR extension are reproduced in our *Branch Lines around Porthmadog 1954-94*. Here we outline the development of services in respect of the number of trains that could be operated simultaneously on the line.

One train covered the timetables until 1958, when Tan-y-Bwlch was reached and an unadvertised afternoon relief train (known to the operators as "The Flying Flea") was run. The two trains met at the new terminus. This additional train departed at 3.0pm from Portmadoc and was advertised in the 1961 public timetable. From 1962, trains passed at Minffordd.

Extension to Dduallt in 1968 brought a three-train service for the first time, passing normally at Minffordd and Tan-y-Bwlch.

The provision of a loop at Rhiw Goch in 1975 allowed crossing of trains there each side of the summer peak weeks, when Minffordd and Tan-y-Bwlch were used. A fourth train set (albeit third-class only) was introduced in 1977 for the peak service to Llyn Ystradau, this being the maximum number of trains to work at any one time. That year, a relief train at 17.00 from Porthmadog was worked on some days, bringing the number of departures to 15 in a day.

After the peak traffic years of the mid-1970s timetables were adjusted down to reflect demand. From May 1988, the peak service was hourly, all trains passing at Tan-y-Bwlch. There were ten departures from each terminus.

Short journeys have been operated on parts of the railway from time to time, notably Tan-y-Bwlch to Dduallt consequent upon reopening to the latter, and Dduallt northwards to allow passengers to view the recently-completed spiral line. Innovations in the 1990s included a Porthmadog-Minffordd shuttle service and a morning Blaenau Ffestiniog - Tan-y-Bwlch return journey.

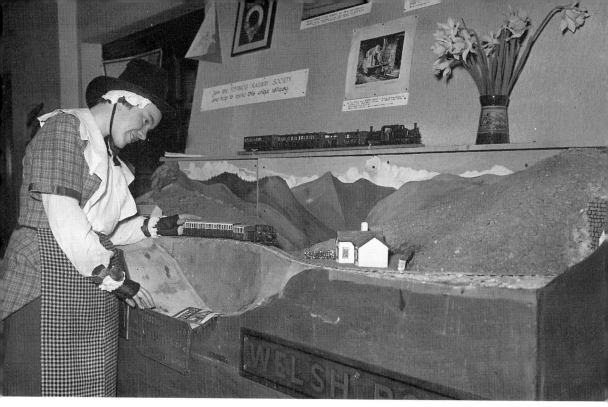

1. The FRS was incorporated as a limited liability company in 1954 and launched its public appeal at the annual Model Railway Club's Exhibition at Central Hall, Westminster, at Easter 1955. The main attraction was Barbara Fisk, masquerading as the famous Welsh-costumed Tan-y-Bwlch station mistress. (Barbara was then engaged to your author (VM) and is now joint owner of Middleton Press). Press photographers were duly attracted, details of the scheme and this photograph appearing, next day, on the front of the daily newspapers in Wales. (V.Mitchell coll.)

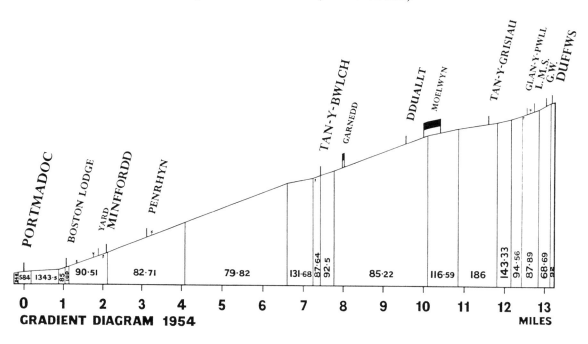

GRADIENT DIAGRAM 1954

F.R. LOADING GAUGES

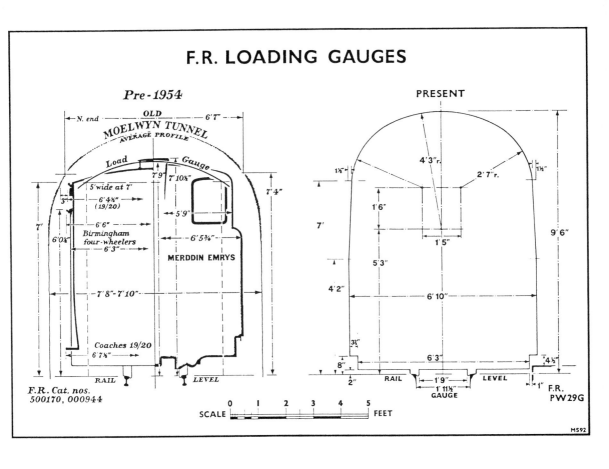

Pre-1954

PRESENT

OLD
N. end | 6'7"
MOELWYN TUNNEL
AVERAGE PROFILE

Load | Gauge
7'9" | 7'10½"

5' wide at 7'
6'4½"
(19/20)
7'4"
3"
6'6"
Birmingham
four-wheelers
6'3"
6'0¼"
5'9"
7'
6'5¾"

MERDDIN EMRYS

7'8"-7'10"

Coaches 19/20
6'7½"

RAIL | LEVEL

F.R. Cat. nos.
500170, 000944

4'3"r.
2'7"r.
1¼" | 1½"
1'6"
1'5"
9'6"
7'
5'3"
4'2"
6'10"
3½"
8"
6'3"
4½"
2"
RAIL | LEVEL
1'9"
1'11½"
GAUGE
1"

F.R.
PW29G

SCALE | FEET
0 1 2 3 4 5

MS92

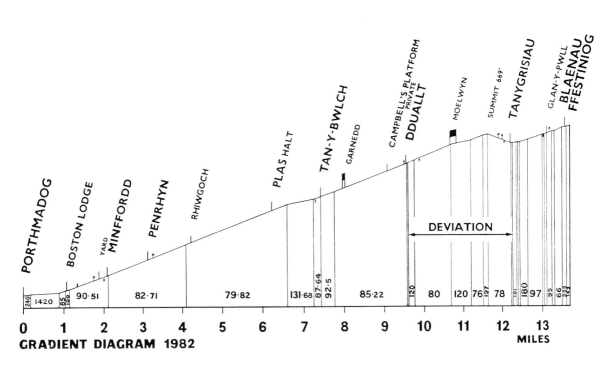

PORTHMADOG
BOSTON LODGE
MINFFORDD YARD
PENRHYN
RHIWGOCH
PLAS HALT
TAN-Y-BWLCH
GARNEDD
CAMPBELL'S PLATFORM PRIVATE
DDUALLT
MOELWYN
SUMMIT 669'
TANYGRISIAU
GLAN-Y-PWLL
BLAENAU FFESTINIOG

DEVIATION

240 | 1420 | 85 | 90·51 | 82·71 | 79·82 | 131·68 | 87·64 | 92·5 | 85·22 | 120 | 80 | 120 | 76·7 | 78 | 101 | 180 | 97 | 95 | 66 | 255

GRADIENT DIAGRAM 1982

0 1 2 3 4 5 6 7 8 9 10 11 12 13

MILES

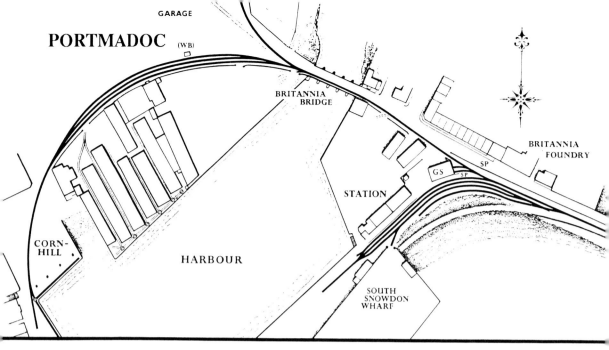

PORTMADOC (WB)

GARAGE

BRITANNIA BRIDGE

BRITANNIA FOUNDRY

GS

SP

SP

STATION

CORN-HILL

HARBOUR

SOUTH SNOWDON WHARF

2. This scene of dereliction greeted visitors in June 1951 although the office was still used by the manager, Mr. Robert Evans, who dealt with such matters as property rents and takeover bids. Rotting on the right is coal wagon no. 18 and in the platform is no. 3, a curly roof guards van which had to be broken up. Victorian tramcar builders described this style as "turtle roof". (A.G.W.Garraway)

3. Four months after takeover, the yard was clearer but the track was very poor. Many slate wagons were cut up on the spot to raise cash but the three-wagon bolster set (right) was retained, although too rotten to use. The unbroken windows reflect the discipline of the period. (CEA)

4. An aerial view on 17th May 1956 includes the station buildings (centre), the deserted Llechwedd Quarry Company's slate storage sheds (left distance) and the empty South Snowdon Wharf (left foreground). The road to the latter is in the foreground of picture no. 2. (A.G.W.Garraway)

5. The rails across the Britannia Bridge over the River Glaslyn once carried trains to the Welsh Highland Railway and also to the slate wharves. (See pictures 56-60 in *Branch Lines around Portmadoc 1923-46*). After takeover they were used by the internal combustion engine (Simplex) to visit the filling station which was opposite the present one. *Prince* was recorded on 2nd September 1958, with a train of recently lifted rails. (N.F.Gurley)

6. One of the events organised on 22nd May 1963 to mark the centenary of steam traction on the FR was a demonstration of horse power. The animal was one of the few still accustomed to such work and was brought from the Nantlle Railway for the occasion. The precise location of the birthplace of the first locomotives (George England's works) is shown after picture no. 24 in our *South London Line* album. (R.Fisher)

FESTINIOG RLY. | FESTINIOG RLY.

FESTINIOG RLY.	FESTINIOG RLY.
Portmadoc (Harbour) to	**Boston Lodge** (For Portmeirion) to
BOSTON LODGE (For Portmeirion)	**PORTMADOC** (Harbour)
Fare as advertised Third Class	Fare as advertised Third Class

Nº 0154   Nº 0154

Issued subject to the Conditions contained in the Company's notices exhibited at their premises.

7. Vast effort had been put into track improvements by the time that this photograph of *Prince* was taken on 24th August 1963. The headboard recorded the labours of the 500th "Tadpole", a term applied to boys from Enfield who worked mainly on line clearance, under the guidance of Keith Catchpole, school teacher and volunteer FR driver for 39 years. (R.G.Roscoe)

8. Seen outside the goods shed in March 1966 is the Tasmanian class K1 0-4-4-0T. This was the world's first Beyer-Garratt locomotive, having been built in Manchester in 1909. It returned to the works upon retirement and was acquired by the FR but never reconditioned or cut down for use. It was transferred on loan to the National Railway Museum in York in July 1976. (N.F.Gurley)

9. Sadly the FR and its passengers had to suffer the effects of a very high density housing development on South Snowdon Wharf. The level crossing in the foreground was closed and a new road (left) laid down, this necessitating track realignment in 1968. Coach no. 11 was converted to an observation saloon in 1957-58 and is coupled to no. 12 which was adapted as a buffet car in 1957. (N.F.Gurley)

10. Further upgrading of the permanent way started in December 1966, when the poorly supported steel plates over the inspection pit (seen in picture no. 6) were eliminated. The bolster wagons were created from old slate wagons, with the bolsters from the wagons seen in picture no. 3. (N.F.Gurley)

11. Work in February 1967 included moving the king points 70ft to create a longer loop and the opportunity for improving sidings later. Lower left is the line linking with the one seen in picture no. 5 and, lower right, is one of the two roads to the former goods shed, which was used briefly for carriage repairs in the late 1960s. (Festiniog Railway Co.)

12.   The local authority chose to ignore historical facts and changed the name of the town, much to the annoyance of some residents, visitors and historians. At this time the station building was greatly extended to give more space for the shop, buffet and offices. The shell was completed in November 1974. (Festiniog Railway Co.)

13.   The attic above the booking office was adapted to house the control office from which public announcements are made and the entire railway traffic and its connections are organised. The 24-hour clock for train times was introduced in 1968.
(Festiniog Railway coll.)

14. In its early years in Victorian times, the FR was noted for its innovation and being at the forefront of technology. This philosophy has been applied again, notably in computerisation of ticket sales and accounts. Embracing the new *Apricot* in 1986, are Norman Gurley (left) and Brian Bushell. The latter was subsequently consulted by other transport undertakings, the FR having been the first to have computerised tickets - BR followed. (R.Hardy)

15. In an increasingly competitive tourist market, the FR is ever vigilant to ensure passenger comfort and satisfaction. It was not until 1987 that funds permitted the construction of a platform canopy to give waiting passengers shelter from the elements. (N.F.Gurley)

16. In addition to the biennial Galas held since 1986, there have been a number of vintage weekends to generate revenue from railway enthusiasts. Coal-fired *Palmerston* was photographed hauling freight and slate wagons across The Cob at one such event on 26th June 1994, the 40th anniversary of the acquisition of the FR by the new management. (V. Mitchell)

17. The Simplex was recorded with coaches 10 and 17 on 24th September 1994, forty years after the same stock had formed the first train to move on the FR after its nine-year closure. The running lines have heavy flat-bottom rail while some sidings retain the old FR double-head pattern. (V. Mitchell)

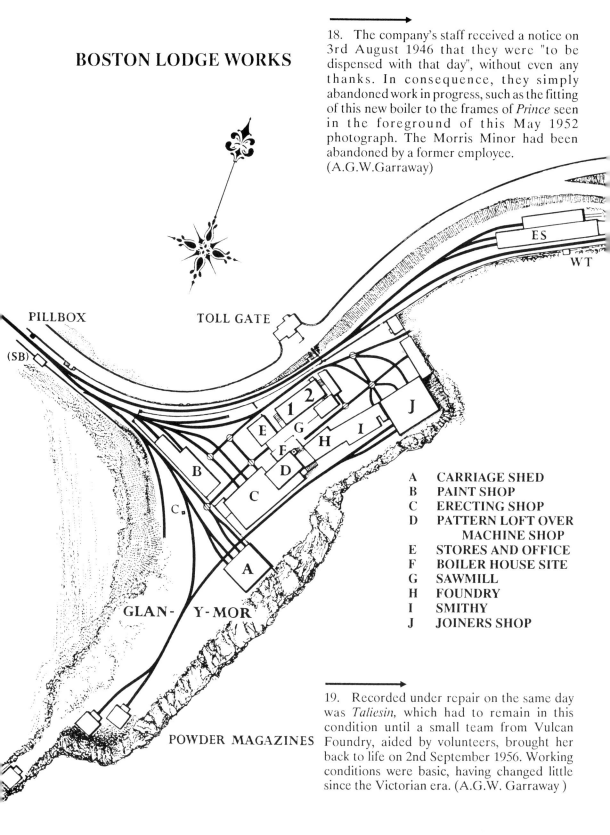

BOSTON LODGE WORKS

18. The company's staff received a notice on 3rd August 1946 that they were "to be dispensed with that day", without even any thanks. In consequence, they simply abandoned work in progress, such as the fitting of this new boiler to the frames of *Prince* seen in the foreground of this May 1952 photograph. The Morris Minor had been abandoned by a former employee. (A.G.W.Garraway)

PILLBOX

(SB)

TOLL GATE

ES

WT

J

E   G   I   H

F   D

B

C

C.

A

GLAN- Y- MOR

POWDER MAGAZINES

A   CARRIAGE SHED
B   PAINT SHOP
C   ERECTING SHOP
D   PATTERN LOFT OVER
      MACHINE SHOP
E   STORES AND OFFICE
F   BOILER HOUSE SITE
G   SAWMILL
H   FOUNDRY
I   SMITHY
J   JOINERS SHOP

19. Recorded under repair on the same day was *Taliesin*, which had to remain in this condition until a small team from Vulcan Foundry, aided by volunteers, brought her back to life on 2nd September 1956. Working conditions were basic, having changed little since the Victorian era. (A.G.W. Garraway)

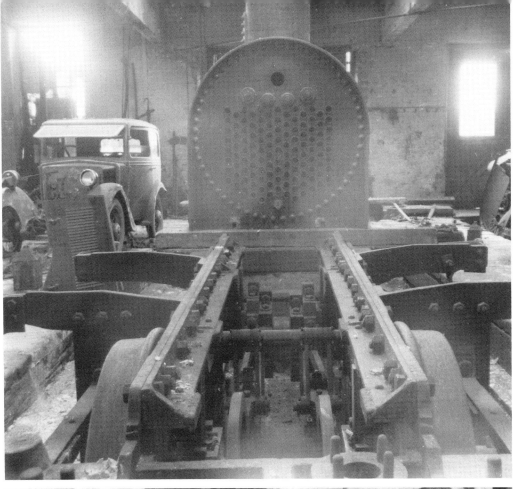

20. The yard was recorded shortly after the keys had been handed over in June 1954. From left to right are the cab and side tank of the single Fairlie *Moel Tryfan*, the hearse (topped with Grecian urns) and coaches 16 and 19, with no. 21 behind the hearse. First, find the rails! The foundry chimney remained standing until 1978. (A.G.W.Garraway)

21. The World War I armour-plated Simplex tractor was started up on 21st September 1954 and driven this far. Further progress that day was prevented by turf growing on the deep sand, blown from the nearby beach. It had settled in the lee of the abandoned coaches, two quarrymens and two of the Hudson tourist type. (A.G.W.Garraway)

22. An October 1954 picture, from almost the same point as the last, reveals that the rails on the main line were clear, this being the case across The Cob to Harbour station. On the right is a World War II defence position (known as a "pill box" and demolished in 1955) and the point levers. These were moved into the shelter (left) which had been a signal box until the Light Railway Order was obtained in 1923. The building was demolished later when the headshunt was extended. (CEA)

23. As no run-round loop was available at Boston Lodge, all trains in the 1955 season were propelled empty from the halt to the yard points. They were uncoupled, attached to a chain and shunted up the main line while the locomotive ran into the yard, as witnessed here. They were then propelled back to the halt to collect the waiting passengers. This was the site of Pen Cob Halt from 1956 until 1967. (J.B.Snell)

24. At the furthest corner of the works from the yard gate was the joiners shop (see plan), its rail access being from two directions. Allan Garraway has taken *Moelwyn* into it along the invisible track from Glan-y-Mor yard. The roof of Glan-y-Mor carriage shed had collapsed on to coach no. 20, making it difficult to retrieve coaches 18 and 20. The smithy chimney is on the left. (N.F.Gurley)

25. A 1956 picture reveals that the joiners had left their tools in place when they left in 1946 and a spare station lamp was still hanging in the roof. The quarrymens coach (by then van no. 2) is on the line from the top yard. The shed was demolished in August 1962, your author having earlier lifted some of the floor boards for use in adapting a slate wagon for the conveyance of locomotive coal. (K.Catchpole)

26. The trackwork of the top yard remained little altered when photographed in November 1958. The nearest van is on the curved line to the joiners shop. To the left of the toll cottage are the substantial gate pillars which marked the point where the main line left FR property and passed onto the Tremadoc Estate, owners of The Cob and the ground on which Harbour station stood. The freehold of the latter was purchased in 1978. (A.G.W.Garraway)

27. When reopened, the works had no mains electricity. A single-phase supply was soon connected but 3-phase for machine tools had to await funds. The overhead shafting was back in action in December 1955, powered by a Crossley engine. Some of the belts driven by it are visible in this March 1960 view of the top power bogie of *Merddin Emrys* in the erecting shop. (A.G.W.Garraway)

28. *Taliesin* was renamed *Earl of Merioneth* in April 1961 and is seen on 21st May 1961 with the works in the background and the partially exposed tracks to the former running shed in the foreground. At that time, this shed was used for storage of coaches and non-functional locomotives. (P.T.Waylett)

29. The FR had wagons of various ancestries. Nearest the camera is an ex-Croesor Railway wagon (FR no. 196). The unusual three-way stub points had been at the south end of Harbour station since 1879 and were moved to this site in Glan-y-Mor yard in March 1964, later being transferred to Minffordd yard. (N.F.Gurley)

30. In an attempt to resolve the locomotive crisis, the FR bought this bulky 1944 Peckett 0-6-0ST from Harrogate Gasworks in 1957 but little work was done on it. It was sold in 1989. Alongside it is a decaying four-wheeled coach, which "fell to pieces in their hands". It was no. 12 in the old numbering.
(Festiniog Railway coll.)

31. Glan-y-Mor yard was gradually cleared of undergrowth and new sidings laid down to serve the Permanent Way Dept. Its main storage area was later established at Minffordd. In the foreground is the roof of the carriage shed which was extended in 1964-67. The long shed was used as a running shed from 1955 until it was demolished in 1988, owing to its deteriorating condition. (N.F.Gurley)

32. Another photograph from the late 1960s shows the top yard as a storage area and a site for caravans to house staff and volunteers, sufficient accommodation being a chronic problem. The long building in the background was the running shed until 1946, a useful sand pit being to the right of it. (N.F.Gurley)

33. Taking shape is the first new locomotive to be built in the works for 90 years and the first new Fairlie for over 60, so claimed the Festiniog Railway Magazine. Confusingly, it was to be called *Earl of Merioneth*. Behind is Alco-built 2-6-2T *Mountaineer* undergoing repair, having been on the FR since 1966. (Festiniog Railway coll.)

34. A July 1979 panorama of the yard includes oil tanks, all working locomotives being oil-fired by that time. On the right is the newly built *Earl of Merioneth*, then just completed utilising old bogies. Centre is *Upnor Castle*, vacuum-fitted for use on passenger trains. (N.F.Gurley)

35. Having the first telephone system in the district, the FR offered a public service and various slate business premises in the towns at each end of the railway were connected to it. This historic equipment is sometimes on show in the works. Left is a five-part unit from about 1895 consisting of a magneto bell, magneto generator, switch hook, induction coil and transmitter. Next is a one-unit telephone from about 1900. Then comes a 16-line exchange from the same era. On the right is a 1923 omnibus magneto telephone from the WHR. In the revival era, a number of unattended automatic exchanges were installed in series along the line but a call from end to end involved dialling two digits for each exchange on the route. The later installation of a tandem exchange at Boston Lodge resolved this problem and capacity was increased. (Festiniog Railway Co.)

36.   Photographed in the erecting shop extension on 20th October 1985 is *Merddin Emrys*, having been dismantled prior to a heavy boiler overhaul. New smokeboxes of more traditional style were fitted to the austere, albeit functional, looking locomotive. (N.F.Gurley)

37.   Continuing the quest for efficiency in narrow gauge operation pioneered by the FR management in the 1870s, the current FR team perfected push-pull operation, seen here in the form of driving trailer no. 111 being hauled past the works by Planet *Conway Castle*. Introduced in 1990, the train is used mainly at off-peak times. (Festinog Railway coll.)

38.   Work started on the new Glan-y-Mor carriage servicing shed in 1991 and here is the result, complete with splendid new trackwork to release engines bringing stock into it. The old carriage shed, in the distance in this June 1994 view, was used as a paint shop. By that date it was the locomotive running shed. (V.Mitchell)

39. A special inspection train was run on 21st July 1955, two days before the reopening. From left to right are Allan Garraway (manager), Lt.Col.McMullen (HM inspecting officer), Les Smith (FR director), Will Jones (platelayer before and after closure), Rev.Timothy Phillips (nearby resident and self-appointed honorary custodian of the works during the closure) and a young witness. (M.Seymour)

40. Rhiw Plas bridge (north of the halt) was rebuilt to carry heavy power station components from the ships at Portmadoc Harbour to Trawsfynydd. It also gave the railway greater clearances. This necessitated the provision of a level crossing for part of 1959 and 1960. Spoil trains were run to Tan-y-bwlch behind *Taliesin*. (N.R.Gurley)

NORTH OF BOSTON LODGE

41.   A works train from Dduallt runs under gravity over the site of the level crossing, the new bridge in the background having opened on 1st June 1960. An embankment slip near the halt in 1954 delayed progress of the pioneers of the line. (N.F.Gurley)

42.   An unexpected problem faced the struggling revivalists here. The MOT inspector required the massive stone gate post to be repositioned further from the track in 1957. New gates were made from the roof timbers of the demolished portion of Glan-y-Mor shed. Quarry Lane crossing soon became known as Lottie's Crossing, after the resident keeper here for over 30 years. It was automated on 28th October 1991; the photograph dates from March 1965. On the right is the quadrant for operating the distant disc signal.
(A.N. Massau)

43. Natural forces, notably strong winds from the west, had done much to create an air of despair in the waiting area. The LMSR had passed into oblivion and the lantern seemed set never to shine again. (J.Fraser)

44. The house remained occupied and the fine tracery of the barge board could still be discerned by the observant. Completed in 1874, the building had a public posting box in its wall from the 1890s to 1915. (J.Fraser)

45. The FR booking office was reopened in 1956 but the BR one was closed a few years later. This 1971 photograph reveals that their fares were collected on the trains by then. BR tickets were sold here for a while from the FR office; they are still sold over the counter (or by post) at Harbour Station to benefit FR funds. (Festiniog Railway coll.)

46. Standing on top of the bridge over BR on 28th October 1978 is a new set of points for the bottom end of the loop. *Moel Hebog* waits to draw them into place by means of a rope. The top points had been moved in 1964 to increase the length of the loop. (N.F.Gurley)

47. Starting in 1957, the FRS ran a number of steam-hauled special trains from London in connection with its AGMs. After an absence of over 20 years, steam returned to the Cambrian Coast line and platform clearances had to be measured again. No. 7819 *Hinton Manor* was recorded on a trial trip on 22nd May 1987, while *Blanche* posed for the occasion. (N.F.Gurley)

48. The Heritage Group has become increasingly active, helping to restore historic stock and structures while also running an occasional demonstration slate train by gravity. Working Party Organiser David High has laid down his horn in order to hand over the single-line token on 25th June 1994. The train terminated in the siding here. Full automatic signalling of this loop was commissioned on 18th March 1989. (V.Mitchell)

MINFFORDD YARD

49. The Simplex and coach no. 10 stand on the curve from the main line on 1st January 1957, while the workers (volunteers from Derby) watch the management (Allan Garraway) repair the then recently excavated points. Most of the tracks in the yard were buried under debris and/or vegetation. (K.Cribb)

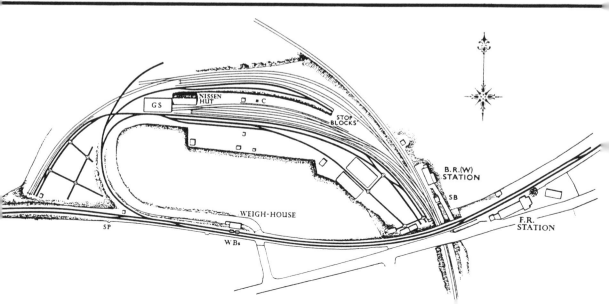

50. *Prince* climbs out of the yard with a load of clean ballast, its exhaust appearing to merge with the clouds. In the background are BR wagons loaded with dirty ballast. A screen was arranged near the coal chute, so that it was "cleaned" during transfer, although clay contamination was often troublesome. (N.F.Gurley)

51. Ex-GWR 3-ton travelling crane no. 542 of 1937 was purchased in 1965. The boiler from *Linda* was lifted onto the company's lorry on 3rd November 1968, prior to transport to Hunslet's Works for fitting of a superheater and new firebox. (N.F.Gurley)

52. In the early 1970s, new ballast began arriving by road from the nearby quarry at Y Garth. Problems such as this arose if the lorry was loaded overnight and part of the load froze into a block. (I.Walsh)

53. The goods transfer shed was leased out as a sawmill from about 1940 to the end of 1964, when it was taken over by the PW Dept. The drilling of high-quality Australian Jarrah sleepers is seen in progress in April 1981. (N.F.Gurley)

54. A BR Matisa ballast tamper was bought in 1968 and a ten-year conversion programme resulted in the creation of this very useful machine, claimed as another "first" for this gauge in this country. By June 1985, it had tamped 25 miles of track and performed 53,665 cycles; by 1990 it had travelled 1782 miles on the line. (N.F.Gurley)

55. Escalating insurance premiums to cover forest fires and other conflagrations caused by engine sparks were becoming an increasing problem. (The FR was first taken to court over the loss of a haystack in 1867). Oil firing was the solution and was introduced in stages - *Linda* 1970, *Blanche* 1971, *Mountaineer* in 1972, the year in which *Merddin Emrys* worked the last regular coal-fired train. About 30% of the fuel used was waste oil, but its use was suspended in 1993 due to its variable quality. (N.F.Gurley)

PENRHYN

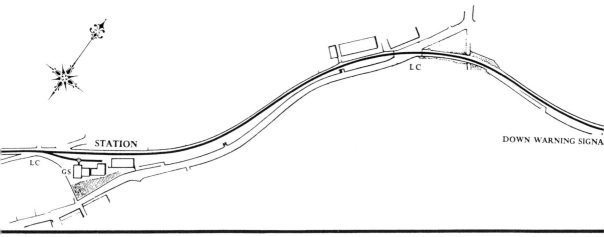

STATION

LC

GS

LC

DOWN WARNING SIGNAL

56. The crossover near Minffordd weigh-house was lifted and its points were used to form a loop here so that in 1957 the station could serve as a terminus. *Moelwyn* waits in the afternoon sun on 10th February of that year. (A.G.W.Garraway)

57. The loop was used for passing trains from 1961. A headshunt was added (between the Austin van and the Wickham trolley) in 1969 to allow long down trains to clear the top points. *Prince* has just reversed onto the unbraked wagons and nudged them over their chocks. Fortunately they were poor runners and did not continue downhill. (N.F.Gurley)

58. Snow was still to be seen on Moelwyn as work started at Easter 1967 on adapting the station to serve as a hostel for volunteers. It was completed in 1971 and was the subject of a major renovation scheme in 1987. Another hostel was established at Minffordd and is visible in the background of picture no. 55. A new capacious bulding was completed there in 1995. (D.H.Wilson)

59. The maintenance and upgrading of the civil engineering structures is one of the less well publicised and appreciated aspects of the company's work. Bridge reconstruction is seen in January 1970 at Capel Nazareth, south of the station. (N.F.Gurley)

EAST OF PENRHYN

60. To enable a new timetable pattern to be devised, an additional passing loop was required and work started in 1973, regular use commencing on 17th May 1975. Timetable revision in 1988 meant that the facility was no longer required but the track was left in place. Replacement of the signals started soon after this photograph was taken in July 1994. (V.Mitchell)

61. Opened on 1st June 1963, the halt has been used mainly by people attending residential courses at Plas Tan-y-Bwlch, the roof of which can be seen from the train nearly one hundred feet below the line. Seen in 1994, the stone-built shelter replaced an old quarrymens carriage body in 1989. Combined rail and admission tickets to the gardens were available from April 1995. (V.Mitchell)

62. A view from the bottom of the loop towards the station points in 1954 suggests that only one line in the long loop was used in the final years of operation. By 1951, the track below here was impassable even on foot (your author tried to penetrate the rhododendron jungle), whereas the route northwards was clear. (CEA)

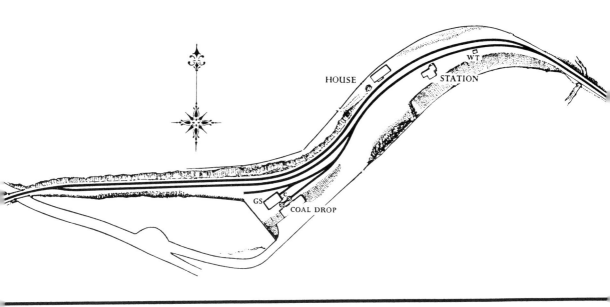

HOUSE | STATION | WT | GS | COAL DROP

63. The top points had been kept oiled during the closure period by Will Jones (former PW foreman), who lived in the station house with his wife Bessie (former stationmistress here). While a terminus (from 1958 to 1968), the station had an informal ambience devoid of fencing and platforms. (P.Burr)

64. Recorded from the top of a tree on 1st August 1966, the station was often very crowded following arrival of trains at 3.00 and 3.35pm. They were timetabled to depart at 3.35 and 4.00. Just in sight is the goods shed, the conversion of which to a cafe took place in 1968. (H.R.Wilson)

65. Track realignment was required before construction of the present island platform could start. It came into use on 27th May 1968, although trains had started running to Dduallt on 6th April of that year. The 1873 station building (right) narrowly escaped demolition at this time and was the subject of a restoration programme in the early 1990s. (N.F.Gurley)

66. An old road tanker was lifted into place on 12th May 1969 to provide greater water capacity. It was in use until 1993. Also featured are the tender cab of *Blanche* and the corrugated iron of the now long-forgotten (and best forgotten) urinal. New toilets were completed in 1971. In the foreground is the works manager, the late Paul Dukes. (A.G.W.Garraway)

67. Fencing arrived in the interests of safety in 1969 and the footbridge was constructed in 1970-71. In the background is the cafe (ex-goods shed), which has had an extension and modern hygienic toilets since 1990. (N.F.Gurley)

68. The 1964 siding near the former goods shed was shortened in 1966 to increase car parking space. Here we witness alterations further west in November 1973. Flat bottomed pointwork is being installed. (N.F.Gurley)

69. Pictured on 24th September 1994 (from left to right) - the new water tank (with traditional-style lamps), the old station (recently renovated), *Prince* (with vintage coaches), the station cottage (unchanged with the passage of time), the signal box (built in 1971, but its lever frame was never used) and the top siding. Full automatic signalling was introduced here on 11th May 1987 after a long period with temporary equipment. (V.Mitchell)

70. The Baldwin *Moelwyn* stops in the midday sun with the weedkiller wagon at the western portal of Garnedd Tunnel. As this structure limits the loading gauge, the enterprising management plan to realign the track close to its original route where the poles stand. (Festiniog Railway Co.)

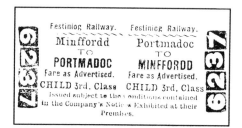

CAMPBELL'S PLATFORM

71.   Colonel Campbell moved to Dduallt
Manor (below the line) in 1963 and became
greatly involved with the deviation which was
started in January 1965. Being a licensed
explosives handler, his services were often in
demand. His barn became a mess for
Deviationists and was in regular use until 1973.
A siding with ground frame was constructed
in 1966 to accommodate the Deviationists'
trolley and the two diesel locomotives that
Colonel Campbell bought in that year.
(N.F.Gurley)

72. The Colonel's locomotives were built by Motor Rail Ltd. (successors to Simplex) in 1940 and received cabs after arrival on the FR. A legal running powers agreement was drawn up (by the Colonel - he was also a solicitor). *Prince* has stopped at the halt in September 1980 with a photographers' special. (N.F.Gurley)

FESTINIOG RAILWAY
PRIVILEGE TICKET PRIVILEGE TICKET
THIRD CLASS THIRD CLASS
Issued subject to the Conditions contained in the Company's Notices Exhibited at their premises.
F76 Williamson, Ashton
0105   0105

FESTINIOG RAILWAY
PORTMADOC to
TAN-Y-BWLCH
FARE AS ADVERTISED
THIRD CLASS PARTY SINGLE
Issued subject to the Conditions contained in the Company's Notices Exhibited at their Premises.
2451   2451

73. Sadly, the Colonel's dream of a fish & chip coach was never fulfilled before he died in 1982. This 1994 view down the line shows the platform edge which remained as a memorial to a remarkable man and great friend of the FR. There was once an aerial ropeway between the platform and the house! (V.Mitchell)

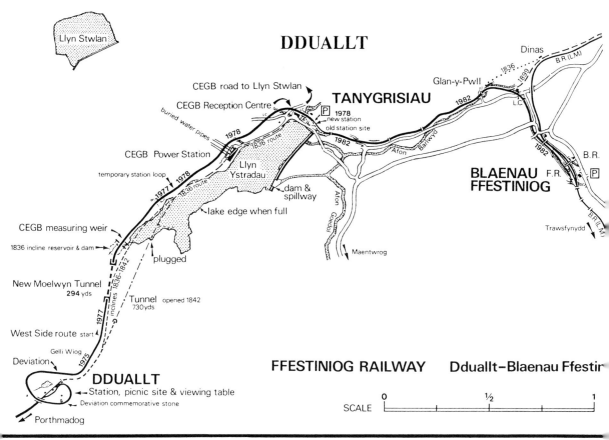

DDUALLT

Llyn Stwlan

Dinas

B.R.(LM)

CEGB road to Llyn Stwlan

CEGB Reception Centre

TANYGRISIAU

Glan-y-Pwll

buried water pipes

1978

1836 route

1978

P 1978
new station
old station site

1982

CEGB Power Station

Llyn
Ystradau

1836 route

temporary station loop

1978

1977

1836 route

dam &
spillway

Afon Barlwyd

1982

1982

BLAENAU F.R.
FFESTINIOG

B.R.

lake edge when full

Afon Goedol

P

CEGB measuring weir

Trawsfynydd

1836 incline reservoir & dam

plugged

Maentwrog

New Moelwyn Tunnel
294 yds

inclines 1836-1842

Tunnel opened 1842
730 yds

West Side route start

1977

Gelli Wiog

Deviation

1975

DDUALLT

Station, picnic site & viewing table

Deviation commemorative stone

Porthmadog

FFESTINIOG RAILWAY   **Dduallt–Blaenau Ffestir**

SCALE 0 ——— ½ ——— 1

74.   The excavation of the cuttings and the construction of the embankments of the spiral part of the deviation were undertaken manually by a dedicated and determined group of volunteers, the turning of the first sod taking place on 2nd January 1965. Skip bodies from a gravel pit near Chichester were mounted transversely, for easy tipping at the ends of embankments. (N.F.Gurley)

75.   Observation car no. 100 (with domestic chairs) ran as part of a clearance test train behind *Prince* on 30th March 1968, before the station opened as a terminus on 6th April following. The loop was not completed until 20th May and a pilot engine had to be available to shunt the train for those few weeks. The mature trees were greatly valued and so the loop was laid to the right of them.
(N.F.Gurley)

76.   The concrete columns were cast and temporary decking was laid on them by eight boys from Westminster School in a single week in January 1969, permanent decking being completed in the following winter. *Moelwyn* is loaded with tools as it runs down the line with a quarrymens coach and three of the early four-wheelers. This train operated a shuttle service between Tan-y-Bwlch and Dduallt between Porthmadog - Dduallt trains.
(N.F.Gurley)

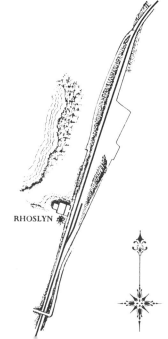

RHOSLYN

77. The repositioned shunting discs are seen in the Spring of 1973, by which time the top ground frame was in use. This controlled the top loop points and access to the old main line, which was used by Deviationists to reach the Tunnel Mess. (Festiniog Railway Co.)

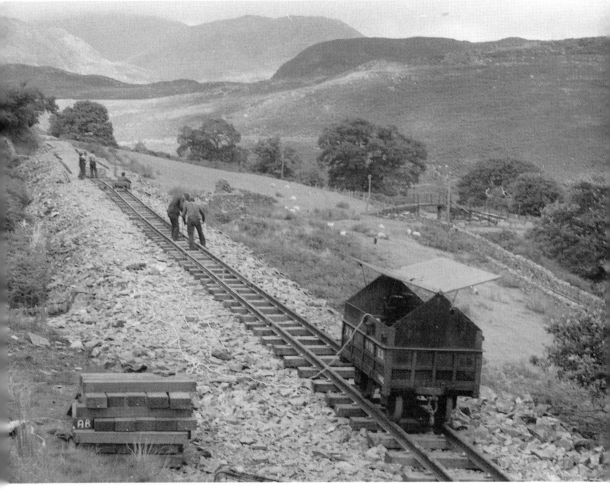

78. Stocks of sleepers were laid down as a temporary platform within the spiral to receive a special train carrying local government representatives and other notables on 7th July 1973. The FR has been successful in securing their support over the years and in obtaining grants from various local, national and European bodies. (Festiniog Railway Co.)

79. The "head of steel" was progressing towards the new tunnel when the new formation was recorded in August 1974; the old line passed under the footbridge on the right. The wagon contains a generator to supply current to the power tools used to speed track assembly. (Festiniog Railway Co.)

80. The spiral line of the deviation commences at the points in the centre of this August 1974 panorama. It gains height through the trees on the left, passes over the old route behind the van, runs in front of the barn on the right and round into the foreground. *Mountaineer* is waiting to proceed from "Spooner's Hollow" down the line with empty ballast wagons and exhausted volunteers. (Festiniog Railway Co.)

81. A wagon stands on the loop seen in the previous photograph. This became a siding after the track on the right was laid to form a longer loop, this coming into use on 1st July 1978. Passengers are gazing at their locomotive as it uses the repositioned top points, which were controlled from the signal box in the background of this picture from July 1979. (N.F.Gurley)

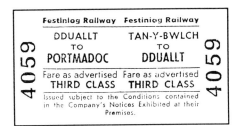

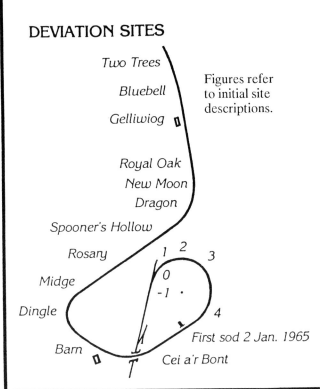

DEVIATION SITES

Two Trees

Bluebell

Gelliwiog

Figures refer
to initial site
descriptions.

Royal Oak

New Moon

Dragon

Spooner's Hollow

Rosary

Midge

Dingle

Barn

2

1

0

3

-1 ·

4

First sod 2 Jan. 1965

Cei a'r Bont

82.   The signal box is on the right of this photograph of *Conway Castle* heading the 08.25 from Porthmadog Harbour on 13th August 1991. The loop and the 13 levers in the box were taken out of use on 15th July 1988 and the signal arms were removed, although the posts for the down signals can still be seen. A ground frame and instrument was installed at the bottom points for the sidings retained for the engineers. The top points were removed to Blaenau Ffestiniog in 1989. (N.F.Gurley)

MOELWYN TUNNEL

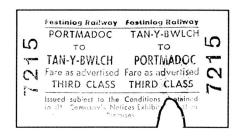

Trains using the old tunnel 1955 - 57
Compiled by Allan Garraway

Date	Loco	Destination	Purpose
1955			
31 January	Simplex	Glan-y-Pwll	Survey
5 February	Simplex	LMR station	CEA meeting
5 March	Simplex	Duffws	Track clearance
23 July	Simplex	Tanygrisiau	Reopening celebration
1 August	Busta	Blaenau	Press officer
31 August	Simplex	Blaenau	Collect wagons
27 September	Simplex	Blaenau	Collect wagons
31 October	Simplex	Blaenau	Collect wagons
1956			
15 March	Simplex	Blaenau	Collect wagons
25 March	Simplex	Tanygrisiau	Director's inspection
9 April	Simplex	Blaenau	Collect poles
28 July	Simplex	Blaenau	Collect wagons
5 August	Moelwyn	Blaenau	Collect poles
6 August	Moelwyn	Blaenau	Collect materials
1957			
12 January	Moelwyn	Lake site	Wagons to CEGB

83. Seen from the north in 1954, the old 730yd long tunnel was straight but gave very little clearance for FR coaches and locomotives. Having walked through it in 1951, your author can confirm that the roof leaked extensively; there were also rotting carcasses of sheep at each end. Rail lifting was completed in 1962. Note that the telegraph pole route went over the hill. (CEA)

84. By June 1975, cuttings at both ends of the proposed new tunnel were ready for underground drilling and blasting to commence. This is the south end, some months later. Three former Cornish tin miners started work on 1st September and achieved break-through on 1st May 1976. (Festiniog Railway coll.)

85. Air-driven water-cooled drills were used to create about 40 eight-foot deep holes, nine of which were close together near the centre of the eight-foot square face. The gelignite in the centre holes was ignited first to create a mass of sand into which rock could be pushed by the other charges. The cycle was as follows- afternoon drill - evening blast - night settle dust - morning muckout. (Festiniog Railway coll.)

86. Subsequently the tunnel was enlarged to about 12ft x 10ft, this almost doubling the enormous tonnage of rock to be transported away. Empty skips are returning to the tunnel in the foreground, having been tipped near the shed, beyond which is an elevator. This conveyed the material on to a screen which separated the fines and the track ballast into wagons standing on the first two sidings, while the large rock dropped into tippers on the third road. (Festiniog Railway coll.)

87. The Simplex (*Mary Ann* from 1971) was fitted with this cab in 1972 and is seen in 1976 shunting wagons of ballast. Also coupled to them is the BEV (Battery Electric Vehicle) which gave pollution-free traction in the tunnel. Members of the Heritage Group removed the roof from the Simplex in 1994 and returned it to its 1954 condition. (Festiniog Railway coll.)

88. Mechanical aids greatly speeded the work in South Cutting, which suffered a severe collapse in February 1976. This is the scene two years later. North Cutting was blasted by contractors but its location in a peat bog caused great difficulties.
(Festiniog Railway coll.)

89. A view in the other direction on 28th May 1977 includes the old route (to the left of the tree), the Tunnel Mess being visible at the end of the line (left) in picture no. 86. *Mountaineer* is at the site of the former screening plant. (Festiniog Railway coll.)

90. Later the same day, *Mountaineer* was to become the first steam locomotive through the tunnel. It is coupled to a bogie wagon on which is mounted a gauging rig; this confirmed that clearances were good. Spirits were high that, after 12 years of toil, trains would run in the Spring. No-one could imagine that, in January, consulting engineers would advise that the tunnel be lined with concrete. None in the district were. (Festiniog Railway coll.)

91. Shotcreting was employed (concrete with plasticiser and accelerator sprayed by means of compressed air). The mixed concrete was brought in by rail and transferred to a pipe-line. The system used was untried; much fell off, spoiling the new track; clearances were lost; rock trimming was required; despondency set in and the opening was delayed until 25th June 1977. The special wagon was hired, the drum rotation being effected by compressed air. (Festiniog Railway coll.)

92. The loading ramp was situated near the site of the future Llyn Ystradau loop. Hire of the special concrete conveyor wagon had ceased by the time this photograph was taken in December 1977. It was replaced by this truckmixer body on a bogie frame. This combination was also used to convey ordinary concrete for such jobs as the signal box base at Dduallt. (Festiniog Railway coll.)

LLYN YSTRADAU

93. The water level in Llyn Ystradau varies with electricity demand and in consequence the water level may be lower than this when summer visitors are here. The run-round loop is seen nearing completion in October 1976. The station was officially open from 25th June 1977 until 24th June 1978, but public services did not commence until 8th July 1977. (Mrs.A.Stephenson.)

94. Blasting was widely used on the new route but seldom recorded on celluloid. This is May 1976 and the construction roadway over the hill is evident. This was largely on the route of the rope-worked inclines which preceded the 1842 tunnel. (Festiniog Railway coll.)

95. Although the railway was open as far as the lake, there was still an immense amount of work to be done, such as drainage channels and landscaping. Here top-soil is being unloaded over-enthusiastically prior to haulage by diesel locomotive *Sludge,* formerly employed at Finham Sewage Works. Some of this work was undertaken by people on a Job Creation Scheme. (N.F.Gurley)

96. "Hidden" costs arose from the demand to construct four 2 ft thick concrete bridges over the underground supply pipes to the power station (right). The concrete is being poured in the Spring of 1977 for the structures that would never be seen. The contract had to be professionally managed (McAlpine undertook it), labour being provided by the Manpower Services Commission. (N.F.Gurley)

97. *Mountaineer* waits at the temporary platform with a special train for tunnel inspection on 28th May 1977. (Note that the equally temporary loop was unballasted and formed of Penrhyn Quarry Railway bull-head rail). The official (and successful) inspection was on the following day.
(Festiniog Railway Co.)

98. Volunteers wait to join a down train at the end of a hot day in 1978. The temporary station having just closed, the platform edge (ex-BR concrete sleepers) was removed and the fence soon followed. An early plan for the deviation took the line to the east of the lake and along the top of the dam in the background.
(N.F.Gurley)

99. The disused loop is in the foreground as the 1979 *Earl of Merioneth* and its train wind past the top of the lake. Tunnel Cutting North is in the background, as are the two remaining sections of the dam of a lake that once provided the power for the pre-tunnel incline by means of a water-wheel. Known as the Archer Dam, it was breached ceremonially on 16th October 1971, soon after the agreement for the west side route had been announced.
(N.F.Gurley)

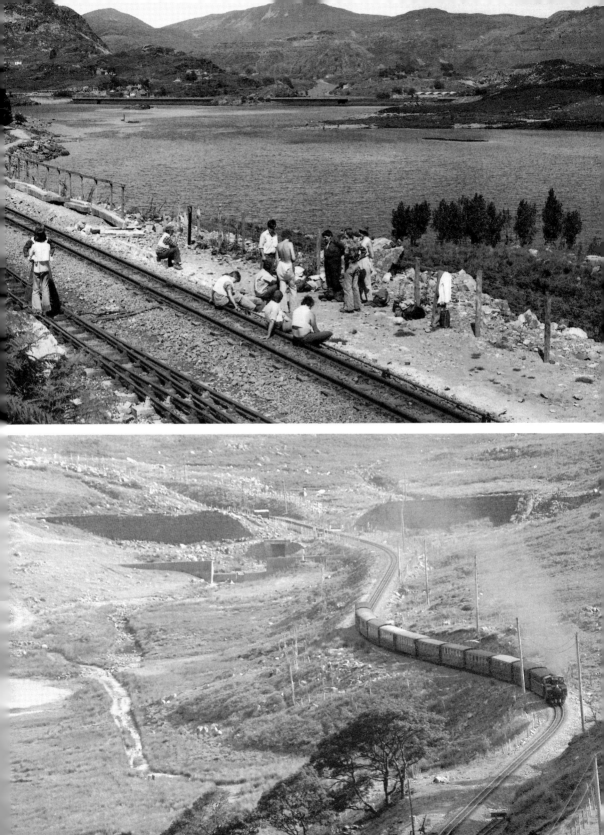

100. Two photographs from the early 1980s show the finished railway near the north end of the lake. Here the dam is on the right and Blaenau Ffestiniog is in the distance. The line crosses two new roads (lower left); curves behind the Power Station Information Centre and enters Tanygrisiau station, the white triangle representing the car park area. (A.G.W.Garraway)

101. A down train crosses Stwlan Dam Road, which climbs steeply to the upper lake. Also on the left are Penstocks Road and its associated crossing lights. The provision of these automated crossings on roads that did not exist when the railway revival started added substantially to the cost of reopening. (N.F.Gurley)

102. Cwmorthin Bridge is on the right of the previous picture and is seen under construction in July 1976. Three lorries arrived on 27th, each carrying a concrete beam 55ft long and 3ft high. After they had been positioned by this mobile crane, there followed the long and intricate job of erecting shuttering and casting concrete round the reinforcing rods. (N.F.Gurley)

TANYGRISIAU

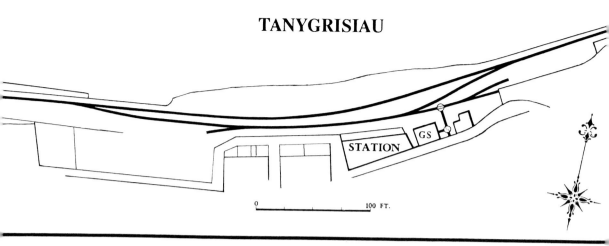

STATION   GS

0   100 FT.

103. Beyond the two-storey station building in this 1952 view towards Blaenau Ffestiniog are the two goods sheds, one of which was still standing (in isolation) in 1994. The new route ends by this goods shed, descending from the summit near the Power Station. (A.G.W.Garraway)

104. Coal arrived here every month in 1946 until July, when the last load arrived and the wagon was abandoned to be photographed in 1954 at the top end of the station. It is also visible in the previous photograph. (CEA)

105. The new station was nearing completion when photographed in March 1978, great efforts being made by permanent staff and volunteers to open the new terminus on time on 24th June 1978. The ruined corner of the old station is to the right of the loop. (N.F.Gurley)

106. By April 1979 the platform had been dressed with tarmac and Cwmorthin Bridge (foreground) had handrails. The shed on the right housed a shop, buffet, booking office and toilets. *Merddin Emrys* is about to return to its train. (N.F.Gurley)

107. The old goods shed (left) gives an indication of the former level of the railway in this vicinity. An immense amount of walling has been undertaken by trained volunteers; here repairs are in progress in the Spring of 1981. Note the temporary water tower. (N.F.Gurley)

108. The new *Earl of Merioneth* has run round its train while passengers use the slope between the car park and platform in the Spring of 1982. Crosville operated buses between Llechwedd Quarry and Stwlan Dam, calling at the BR station in Blaenau Ffestiniog and here. At peak times, additional vehicles such as this double-decker, operated between the latter two points. (N.F.Gurley)

109. The loop was lifted in May 1984. A view from an up train on 23rd July 1994 reveals the steps being taken to reinstate it. The signal box was complete and housed the former Dduallt frame. The track had been laid in a temporary position to facilitate the unloading of material for landscaping part of the car park area. (V.Mitchell)

110. The bridge over the road to Dolrhedyn (the houses of which are visible in the background of picture no. 101) had been demolished in 1957 by the local authority, which was obliged to reinstate it. A constructional error resulted in its being built one foot too high. The railway now has an unwanted hump for evermore. The new span was recorded in December 1979. (N.F.Gurley)

111. Another costly problem presenting itself in this area was rock stability. A fall of rock demolished a kitchen at Pen Craig in November 1975 but did not affect the trackbed. Extensive investigations resulted in a programme of rock bolting, work on this being recorded at Penlan in July 1980. (Festiniog Railway Co.)

112. A 1974 panorama includes one of the many footbridges that had to be rebuilt or repaired prior to reopening. The trackbeds in the right foreground once linked with the Dinas branch and were soon to be buried under slate waste as part of a scheme to beautify the area. (A.G.W.Garraway)

113. Barlwyd Bridge (right of centre in the previous picture) had its abutments repaired and this new decking of old rails applied as part of "Project Blaenau" in 1981. Each project was headed by a leader who organised working parties and materials. (N.F.Gurley)

114. Some industrial archaeology was undertaken at Glan-y-Pwll in 1976 when the locomotive turntable pit came to light. It was probably last used in 1923 and was covered over again as the area became part of the civil engineering depot. (G.Hall)

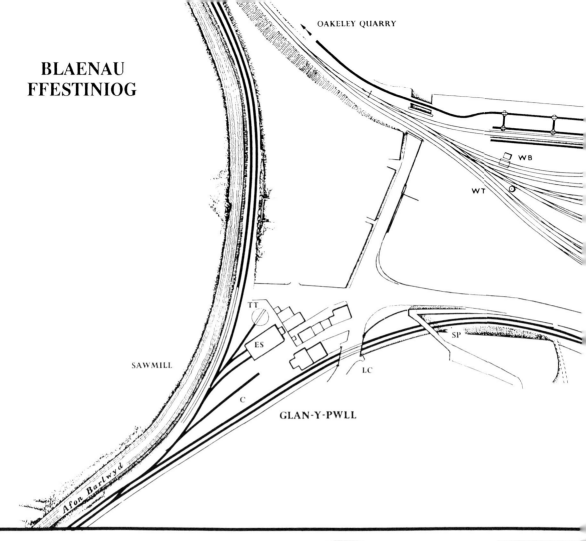

BLAENAU FFESTINIOG

OAKELEY QUARRY

WB

WT

TT

ES

SAWMILL

SP

C

LC

GLAN-Y-PWLL

Afon Barlwyd

115. Adjacent to the LMS station, the FR had a platform with by far the longest canopy on the line. It was sold to serve as a football stand at Manod. Also included in this westward photograph from 21st June 1951 is the single short siding and the water tower. All the rail from here to Tanygrisiau (except at the level crossing) was lifted in the early 1970s, fresh flat bottomed rail (some of it new) eventually replacing it. (V.Mitchell)

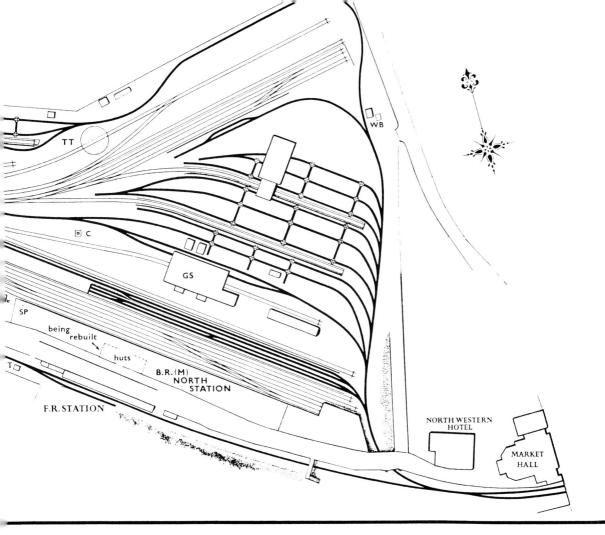

116. An eastward view from almost the same point as the last photograph includes the gable of the North Western Hotel which is also visible in picture no. 118. Dusk is approaching as Enid Catchpole checks the slate wagons, destined for scrapping at Portmadoc, before departure at 4.45pm on 31st October 1956 behind coach no. 10 and the Simplex. (K.Catchpole)

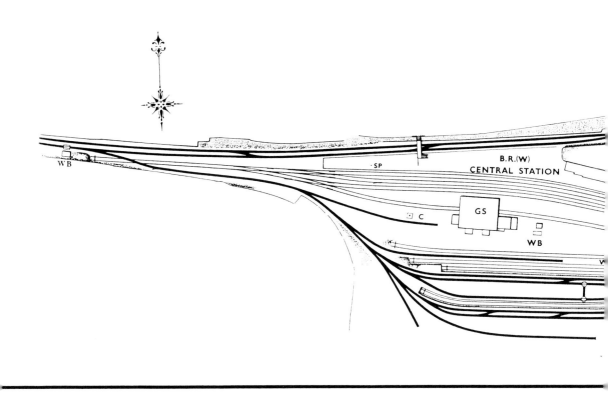

WB

SP

B.R.(W)
CENTRAL STATION

C

GS

WB

117. An April 1961 westward view shows that part of the FR which linked the two stations and which remained in use during the nine-year closure of the rest of the FR. This section carried slate from the Maenofferen Quarry to the BR (ex-LMS) yard until 2nd November 1962. The end of the former GWR line from Bala Junction is on the left. (J.L.Alexander)

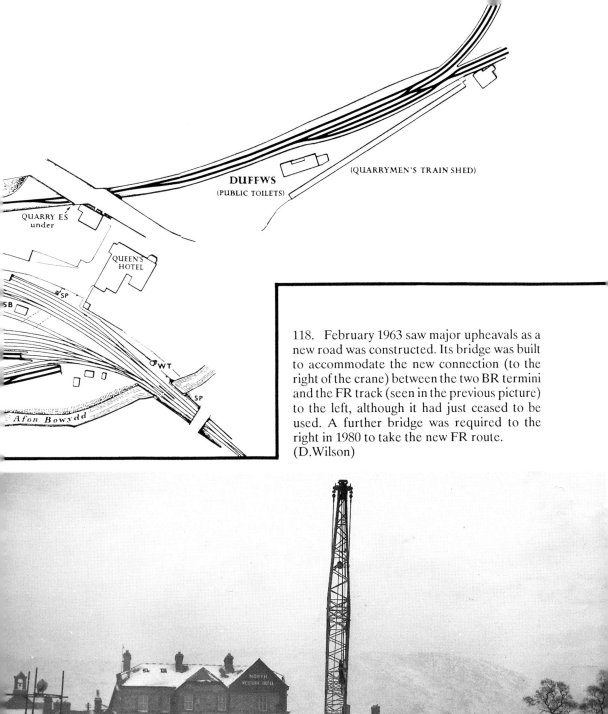

QUARRYMEN'S TRAIN SHED

DUFFWS
(PUBLIC TOILETS)

QUARRY ES
under

QUEEN'S
HOTEL

SP

SB

WT

SP

Afon Bowydd

118. February 1963 saw major upheavals as a new road was constructed. Its bridge was built to accommodate the new connection (to the right of the crane) between the two BR termini and the FR track (seen in the previous picture) to the left, although it had just ceased to be used. A further bridge was required to the right in 1980 to take the new FR route. (D.Wilson)

119. A new joint station, close to the town centre and on the former GWR site, was opened for BR trains on 22nd March 1982 and the FR made a triumphant entry with special trains in the following May, regular services commencing on the 25th of that month. Bearing the headboard "Robert Francis Fairlie 1885-1985", *Earl of Merioneth* runs past the temporary buildings on 1st May 1986. (Festiniog Railway Co.)

120. Permanent buildings and a canopy were completed in the early part of 1990. The spare platform was provided for a possible shuttle train service to the two quarries that are open to tourists. (Festiniog Railway Co.)

121. Double-engine *David Lloyd George* of 1992 runs round its train on 23rd July 1994. BR also entered the heritage business by reintroducing an old-style DMU and repainting it in 1950s livery for the Summer season. All those involved with the Festiniog Railway over the forty years covered by this album have shown the same enterprise and imagination that the creators of this "great little railway" had done over a century earlier. Long may it receive the support it deserves from its staff, volunteers, supporters and passengers alike. (V. Mitchell)